To Paul,
for soul brotherhood
James

Poems
from the Wild River
of Life

James Collins

James Collins

Original title
Poems from the Wild River of Life

Cover design
Sonja Smolec

Layout
Yossi Faybish
Sonja Smolec

Published by
Aquillrelle

ISBN 978-1-329-98793-7

Foreword

In James Collins' book of poetry *Poems from the Wild River of Life*, we are presented a door that opens into the spirit and soul of Collins, but also provides a portal into our own. These poems are the work of someone who listens to nature and to the tolling bells of the soul, often bells of beauty and insight but also of anguish and doubt.

There is something of shimmering moonlight in these poems as well as something tremulous lingering in the shadows that renders the writing both mystic and intimate and makes it difficult to know where the poem ends and our own thoughts begin. Collins understands the honest heart and writes about it in ordinary language that turns on a dime to the magical. *Poems from the Wild River of Life* takes us on a wild ride through rapids and drops us into calm waters. I keep returning to the poems and find new depths in the eddies and in the profundity of the main currents. Read it, you'll be amazed.

~Earl LeClaire, poet, raconteur, author of *Below the Mayonnaise Factory*

Table of Contents

Poems from the Wild River of Life

Discovering A Heaven

My first voyage into the spiritual
came at age 10.
Stepping into a little blue boat, I
pushed off from a lake shore
into my first heaven.

Meeting the water with my hand
on the rudder, I opened the sail
and prayed for wind. A ball of
air turned me into a bolt
over the smooth, liquid

glass tacking silently. I sailed
over the sun, dodged the jib
and left a trail of shredded
cloud reflections in my wake.

For hours my vessel filled
its sail with sky and I
floated in the quiet,
closer to peace.

James Collins

Rite of Passage – Modern Version

I came into the game of life
under the rules of the Old School.
Toss him in. Sink or swim.
That's how they learn.
Not to swim really, but to
deal with fear, betrayal and how
parents can wound you.

A trusting child puts on a swimsuit
by himself for the first time.
With chlorine biting his nose,
squeals of fun and splashes outside
turns Aunt Rose's pool party
into a struggle with self-esteem.

Mumbling about no one helping,
the boy trembles with fear, hoping
he can twist the door knob open.
Squinting through the bright sun, he
sees mom and dad near a barbeque grill.
A tipsy uncle places his beer can down.

That bully of a cousin laughs and
announces your suit's on backwards.
Arms pick you up, strip away your green
inner tube and toss you in the air.
No one hears your screaming bubbles
as you breathe in a shock of water
where air use to be.

If he holds on to degradation, he'll
sink like a stone or live life
stuck as an emotional victim.
Flailing madly in the chaos, he
reaches the pool's edge, saves himself,
and passes this clumsy initiation.

The primal twist in this rite of passage
keeps you from noticing whether
mom or dad were ready
to step in and save you.
And by doing that,
scar you even more deeply.

James Collins

One Wild Ride

Outside the local A&P stood the
galloping palomino horse ride.
It only cost a quarter.
The cowboy in me wanted to
roundup a posse.
The golden mane beckoned and
black reins begged to be held.

But my impatient,
needing-to-cook-dinner mom
won't spare the time or the coin.
Maybe I could rustle some
inner smiles by pretending.
Unsettled with no time for distraction,
mom said, 'You might fall and get hurt.'

She yanked me off the curb, back
into her version of the real world.
Pulled to the car, I glanced back once,
climbed in next to a crinkling
paper sack of groceries.
She closed the harsh, metal door.

Once home, I hopped on my bike,
down the street to play until the
sun sank and the sky shook
out all the pale blue.
One by one friends were
called home to supper.

Alone in the maroon moment
that lost horse ride and lost joy
rose in me like an angry shadow.
Grabbing the handle bar reins of
my imaginary palomino, I
mounted my bike, and
galloped home in a wild ride
through a furious, dusty
cloud of forgiveness.

James Collins

A Magic Tree

Venturing into a foreign land, my
'riding bike' explorers and I found
a magic tree,
casting a spell like Merlin with
elbow bending branches close enough
to earth for brave boys to climb.

This Neanderthal totem easily
enchanted when slow summer days
lasted forever.
The sheer size of this cathedral of
mystical shade bewildered me.

Up close the woody skin was
scarred with carved initials
from ghosts.
My hand ran along the bare bark,
reading the Braille with my
fingers while a rhapsody of rustling

leaves sang soft hymns in the choir loft.
Under the surface of seeing, these
ragged writings
told stories where a love once stood,
where a scavenger in time found a
kiss or a naked body part was revealed.

I was humbled not knowing the tree's name.
Butch, wrestling up a branch, called it
a giant banyan.
Holy artifacts littered the ground.
A cheap, dime store tube of lipstick, a
dull, rusted knife and empty RC cola bottles.

These relics spoke to me like religious
parables, of life, of secrets, of
love and mysteries
from the edge of a world
I did not yet know.

James Collins

Sudden Changes

On the day after
a neighbor's funeral, I
looked out a window into the
sun of a chilly morning and
saw the widow's black dress
hanging on her clothesline.
The crisp, blue sky slowly
turned gray, and soon a
baby powder snow gently
swirled like a
softly shaken snow globe.
As silent as smoke
the feathery flakes
rested on skyscraping trees, and
covered the ground like a
cool, white bed spread.
In this pearl landscape, the
neighbor's funeral dress,
swayed in the breeze
black, untouched and
alone.

Ancient Ruins

In the perfect picture of a summer day
a small gang of boys ride bikes
under a blue sky that flows
like water into forever.
Stopping to explore a park
in some far-off neighborhood,
we scout the terrain like rebel raiders
about to plunder a Federal depot.
We stand straight and tall like
young, fresh hills trying to be mountains.
When the sun reaches the afternoon
boiling point, our bare feet begin to
burn on the rocks and sand.
Racing back to our bikes
where our shoes dangle
from the handle bars like
magical amulets
or scalps,
we ride off like wild Indians
on a buffalo hunt.
Discovering a secret creek, we
explore it with the passion of Lewis & Clark.
As we wade into this new, cool heaven,
in this small, secret river with
almost a waterfall, no one
notices the white mist that
floats around our hearts –
the perfume of innocence.

James Collins

Mosaic

It's not important that Mrs. Marcin, my
seventh grade teacher, lived across the street
with a small, backyard cabin filled with
boxes, bowls and shelves of collected,
catalogued rocks, gems and artifacts.
What is important? One of her assignments
changed my life:
> Stake a three foot square of earth. Observe
> what happens for 15 minutes a day. Write
> a three page report. Due in a week.

How boring, staring at dirt and grass. My
quick plan was write large and skip lines.
The empty corner lot across from my
friend's house would allow me not to miss
any neighborhood baseball games,
bike races or mischief.

Glancing at my random spot, I discovered
a fascinating array of sizes, colors and
shapes doing the business of being bugs.
Some were lost, searching, hunting,
dealing with wounds or obstacles.

A safari of red ants paraded up and
down long shoots of grass toward their
hilly homes outside my perimeter.
I drew the scary creatures with pinchers,
a beetle with turquoise and gold armor, and
what in the hell is that?
Not wanting to miss anything, I scribbled
notes, then looked up.

Neighbors bickered over a fence, cars rolled
through our cobble stone neighborhood, dogs
barked in the distance, and somehow, my
pre-teen, 'star in my own movie' days ended.
I wasn't any kind of main character.
I'm just a little piece, a bit player
in his square of random earth,
lost and learning lessons
in this organic work of art,
this grand, living mosaic.

James Collins

Hot Rod Dreams

In the slow summer of black and white days
when fresh Beatle songs spilled out
every kid's window, I had hot rod dreams.
When I took the rite of passage
from boy to man, the first car I owned
was a '57 Chevy, solid white, black interior.
I quickly christened my ride The White Cloud.

My worn tires soared wildly all week
on a dollar's worth of gas.
Speed impressed. Gas was cheap.
My two-door ticket to freedom had a
simple engine that tuned up easily with
points, plugs and condenser for 20 bucks.
Cars ruled in the kingdom of cool
like powerful wizards

But, cruising drive-ins with bravado for
burgers and babes were flickering images,
fading like the last splices in a
super-8 projector called the old days.
As the king of clouds raced down Central
Avenue, the evil curse of 'Too Good a Deal'
lurked in the pumping pistons.

Within months puffs of black exhaust fumes
began, followed by a darker cumulus haze.
All my fantasies froze when wounded
piston rings seized up and the engine died.
As a junk heap in my parent's yard, I
watched the subtle bruises of rust and the
shine on my youth fade, slowly,
the way all white clouds disappear.

One day my older brother's friend
hauled it away.
I couldn't watch or let anyone
see my tears.
With the White Cloud gone
there was more yard to mow.
I never again gave a
car I owned a name.

James Collins

The Best Star

In the daily ceremony of dawn
the black night quietly transforms
into shifting shades of blue.

In a holy procession from violet,
to pink, then to clear gold
is how the best star pours
the alchemy of light into the world.

This glass of sky fills me with a
joyful wonder with or without
ice cube clouds in the drink.

As I sip this new day pouring
over to wake up life, the
disappearing sky of diamonds
slowly shakes the shadows
out of dusty trees.

I let every whispered kiss of
first light touch me softly.
A sacred breath, no, more of a gasp
escapes from my heart.

Better than any alarm is the silent
music of a beautiful sunrise,
especially when accompanied
by the coo of doves, or a
chorus of bird songs.

Every day my favorite star
warms this silvery blue essence
and holds this chalice of air
that fills with our
dreams and desires.

James Collins

Bars

My heart prefers to avoid
that thick air where desperation
lingers, loneliness dances with
anger in a temporary freedom
found for the price of two drinks.

Even without smoke, bars are
where hearts sour, search and
stare into drinks, wondering
where their life went or when
their puzzling pain will numb.

Those phantom human ships who
drop anchor and dock alone
at bar stools scare me the most.
Each carries a dead dream, tight
as skin, yet loose as clown clothes.

Caressing a burden like a tender lover,
they cling to their glass, a counterfeit
compass that leads nowhere.
In the slow lift of the drink they see
the fool they were, and mutter to

their watery reflection for answers.
But the liquid face of that fool is
wise enough not to speak. Sipping
on 'why can't my life work' or
drowning in the 'who am I' riddle,

barstool ghosts negotiate romances
with promiscuous secrets, whispered
into unfaithful ears, and miss what's
hidden behind the distractions, beyond
mind games, and buried under pretenses.

True meaning is never found because
answers float in a different darkness.
But, as the regulars lift the icy
hammers of tomorrow's hangover
and buy another round,
the band plays on.

James Collins

On The East Side of Innocence

Doing my midnight in Manhattan pace,
I wander through a dark, unknown,
stone forest of skyscrapers.
Stepping a block or two away from a
crowded, noisy street, I begin to
hear only the tapping of my steps.
This lonely sonar echo tells me
I made a wrong turn.
Near the corner of lost and found,
Bowery bums litter the sidewalk
like speed bumps.

Stunned and at a dead stop, I cling
to my life preserver of naiveté until
my eyes register what I really see.
Snoozing sculptures in terrified postures
litter this street-long concrete mattress.
Could the icy indifference of these
broken souls propped in doorways
really decorate this city?
Slowly stepping through the steaming
veils of barren nightmares, my tangled
heart melts in a puddle of compassion.
'What can I do?' screams in my head.
I rummage, but find little
hope in my pockets.

Unable to beg or testify,
some sleepers drool in gutters.
Others snore on ragged shoe pillows.
Walking past me through this cemetery,

native New Yorkers step over them
without breaking their conversation.
Cuddling exhausted bottles in crispy,
brown blankets, these fallen,
frozen gargoyles stir a sizzling
fire in my own dying and
dreaming eyes
now,
cracked marbles
oozing
twin rivers of tears
on the east side of innocence.

James Collins

A Journey

I am the son of a chief no one knew.
He wore no buffalo skins or amulets.
He taught by letting me walk through
the deserts of this world to discover
my own thirst and hunger.

Seeking answers outside the blankets
of knowledge others slept under, I
turned down a crooked, little path, and
found birth, death, love and fear are
all petals on the same flower.

Stumbling alone through misty
illusions of wild fame, I searched
for a heart, for a self, and for my soul.
Six strings on a guitar kept me alive
with waterfalls and rivers of music.

Playing bass took me to many stages
where I could avoid the spotlight.
My breath through a flute has
lifted me into many heavens.
But on this earth, adopted by wolf and

owl, I howl at the moon with my longing.
My owl eyes see in the dark
of every heart a dim, flickering spirit, a
dancing shadow or subconscious candle
wanting to light a fire, or spark a love.

On this road I've hunted for ways to
keep my heart open and my soul free.
Who will know if I succeed or fail?
Whether I'm crushed or ascending I'm
now contented to sing my heart song,
finally.

Ignored by passing crowds of silent,
searching, or sleeping hearts, I
follow the spiritual scent of life,
walking alone and unnoticed,
the son of a chief no one knew.

James Collins

Sack of Stars

After a week of tossing and
turning,
twisting sheets and
pulling covers off and
on, I stopped wrestling
this holy longing.

One night I broke a hole
in the sky and
crawled through.
I grabbed a few stars,
collecting them in a sack.

The next day I showed these
little sparks of spirit
to my friends,
telling them the secret.

That no matter how
far away,
spirit is
more real than the
real we knock on is real.

Looking into my sack of stars,
they shrugged
unimpressed.
I guess it's easier to see
flash and fire
in the dark.

Like many of us,
even stars
lose their shine
in the raw yellow of morning.

James Collins

On The Beach of Heaven

Warm sea air whispers as
gently as a baby dreaming.
A few blankets and crumbling castles
grow out of the bumpy sand.
Sifting silica with my fingers, I stare
into the holy art of land, sea, and air.
If this sky were a two way mirror,
could a human god and the spirit version
see themselves in these granules of life?
Cloud wrinkles disguise the eye of a
God who stares into this world as I
stare out of my human molecules.
Behind this sheer, blue drapery
hides a dark, ancient space
where stars and galaxies roam.
Like a dazed lover I dig into the
flesh and bones of the past, for a clue,
for a message, for some meaning while
clouds stretch in and out of animal shapes,
and dissolve under the gaze of a lazy sun.

Wrapped in towels passers-by dance
across the hot sand, speak in dialects
of suntanned bravado that fly away
like seagull gossip.
Reconnecting with the soothing
voice of my inner ocean, I sit in awe
at this altar in life's cathedral.
In such a mystery I know all I
can do is rearrange the sand.
I'm lost on this toy of earth, in this

puzzle started by some forgotten God
who buried love here long ago.
Not finding it, we keep being reborn
to search for it.
This rebirthing game keeps the planet
spinning and life forever in motion.
I sense that if the prize is no where
outside, the treasure must be within.
In that moment, in the sands of the
here and now, I know when I find
my lost piece of this puzzle, I
will step from this world
on to the beach of heaven.

James Collins

Wondering

'Enjoy not knowing,' says the old Buddhist
monk, so frail that the wooden ruler he idly
taps across his palm looked like a club.
He paces by a teary tank where gold fish
sway in lazy, looping laps. I wonder...
do they have any dreams beyond the
fluttering ecstasy when it rains fish food.

One goldfish darts by a sunken treasure chest,
kisses the ornaments for good luck or long life.
Fish don't start a war if one worships
the filter's magic bubbles. I wonder...
when fins scrape the walls of their watery
home if they believe God is glass.

Clearing his throat the sage says, 'Path is
not in answers, but in questions that crack
the ego open to accept the mystery.
What do you need?' He let our minds kick up
a confusing dust and our brains compile.
'Air should be the only item on list.'

A goldfish rises to the surface, I wonder
will he jump out to taste the next world.
Religion leaves me thirsty. Preferring the
wine of spirit over the dregs of dogma, am I
swimming within my God in life's aquarium?

But like a fish outside his world gulps for water,
my ego gasps for survival, stirs up questions
to answer or a mob of fears when I meditate.
Stuck in the revolving door of breath I spin
with no way out of the mind chatter.

All masters say being spiritual is simple.
None of them say it's easy.
I wonder if enlightenment
comes from a cocoon, it
must be a terrorizing thrill
when the ego shell cracks.
At a threshold of a new opening, I
wonder will the next moment bring
a freedom, a discovery or a death?

'Aren't they all really the same?' the master says,
looking through me as if staring at a goldfish.

James Collins

Careless

I realized this morning there's
no chess set in my house.
Once upon a time a board was
always set up, ready for any
spur-of–the–moment game.

I recall a part-time love with a some
time girlfriend was running on fumes.
She stopped by with her son for the
delicate 'this is going nowhere' ceremony.

Losing his chess teacher, the angry
child left the room. The next morning
there was an empty red square.
A black knight had disappeared.

Dare I make trouble or stir up false
hope? Facing love or danger, the knight's
cavalier two steps forward, one step
sideways left me as empty as my board.

I know the right moves in games
of precision, consequences and no
do-overs. In love's game, no clue. Stuck
in a stalemate, I pondered my next move.

My board was wounded, could only
be played with a salt shaker
substitute, a toy soldier or a lame,
bolt on a lug nut for a recruit.

The empty square looked like
that place in my heart where
people fall in and out of my life.
Even if only AWOL, a piece was gone.

Officially missing in action, the
black knight could never capture
a queen or be taken by one.
Daily inspecting the board, I stared

at this hole in black and red squares.
Hiding a deeper issue of playing it safe,
I half-hoped the knight would gallop
from behind the philodendron.

One day I swept the broken
black horse from under my couch.
Mourning a death by a child's angry toss, I
glued the horse together, but it never held.

The wounded black knight's wild ride
ended in a mass grave of pawns and
bishops, covered with the sacred
dust of a young boy's hurt feelings.

For years
I have not played
the game
one can never
hope to win
by being
careless.

James Collins

Baseball

1
A metaphor for life where a haze of boredom hides
subconscious layers of tactics, crazy hand signals from
third base coaches, silent corrections by dugout
managers on pitch and location.
This deceptively subtle game becomes a sleepy
routine until the crack of a bat. Filled with risk and
uncertainty, bold swings and digging for second, this game
tests you to stay awake because anything can
happen by anyone, at any time, just like life.

2
Only a game? Tell that to Ralph Branca.
A forgotten promise for the Brooklyn Dodgers
in 1951. With 13 wins, 3 shutouts and
striking out 118 that year, he got sent in to
save the pennant winning game in the
bottom of the ninth with two men on and the
winning run at the plate. That's when the Giants
Bobby Thompson hit a home run to steal the
pennant away from the Dodgers.
All the king's horses and all the king's men
could never put Branca back together.
That's a lesson of how one pitch, like a
single choice shatters a man's spirit.

3
For most boys to throw and bat becomes braided
to a father's love, to camaraderie and teamwork.
Once upon a time a boy's heart took the shape of a baseball.
One ties history to it. Lindbergh flew the Atlantic
the same year Babe Ruth hit sixty homeruns.

Figuring batting averages improves math skills.
Seeds of responsibility sprout by learning when to
cover second and when to be the cutoff man.
The smell of an oiled rawhide glove, the risk in
stealing and the jolt of power when bat
meets ball lives in the psyche of most men.
On this small Eden of grass and red clay
the athlete lives in a paradise of hits and runs.
Black and white newsreels don't convey tensions of destiny.
But one can still see Ted Williams swing
and daring taunts of Jackie Robinson leading off base
on the only diamond a guy loves.

4

In the epic balancing of strikes and balls, baseball is sacred.
Records are the Holy Grail. In my mind to break Babe Ruth's record,
hit more homeruns in the same number of games and
seasons as the Great Bambino. Then there is no controversy.
Not in ten more games a season, or in ten more seasons.
Break Ruth's record and I'll waive any requirement that that
player drink as much beer and whiskey as Ruth.
Whether we compare ourselves to anyone
with some asterisk qualifier, I can't say. But in life and baseball,
all I know is the big game is best played by
those willing to risk disaster.

James Collins

Become the Rose

Walking through this world,
    we occasionally
        see a rose bush.

What we do next speaks
    loudly about
        who we are.

        Do we walk by, barely noticing the flowers?
            Too busy with more important things.

        Do we pick a rose to brighten our dull life?
            Then, in a few days throw it in the trash.

        Do we stop and smell the fragrance?
            Enjoy the moment or a memory.

Or,

do we become the rose, giving our
fragrance freely to life.

Lost in Translation

Imagine the mind of that semi-naked
Native American quickly working
through his shock and awe,
watching intruders swarm on shore
from alien water craft to plant flags,
bellow in gibberish and lust for gold.
He had to be irritated, his day being
ruined by hairy, smelly explorers
dressed in sweaty tin can regalia.
After months at sea how bad did they smell?
Who translated this collision of cultures
and deciphered that native's arm
pointing off into the distance?
Maybe he was saying,
'Get your asses off my beach!'
Did he tire of their attempts to weave a
magic spell by waving bright,
thin coins in his face?
Maybe he imagined them as gods, or
was he just eager to be rid of the
clanking conquistadors?
That night the native probably laughed
around the campfire with his story
about making the bearded strangers
vanish with bad directions to the
fantasy of a fountain of youth or
cities of gold so easily believed.
How did he not see the trouble that
would come and did he ever regret
not killing them on the spot?

James Collins

Blindness

Awakening behind curtains, I can't
see any colors in the morning sunrise.
'Oh God!' I swear as I blink my way
from one theater of dreams to another. I
rub the eyes that still only see dark facts.

Shuffling down the drive in the cool
early to get the paper, I'm so sure
the sky is blue, I don't look up or pay
attention to a posse of cardinals searching
wet grass for breakfast even when a
dove warns them to fly off.

Ignoring any cursive words written
by clouds, I'd rather search for God,
for love, or drift in the simple business
of being, but I'm stuck in the deep
trance of a world in chaos.

Loving life, this earth and all I am
used to sing loudly in my heart, but
that song has transposed itself into a
meek melody of murmurs
I dare not sing.

Stumbling back up the drive I
realize some day I won't go
to work or even stand here.
On that day I will dress nothing,
pack only prayers and

with all I've become
vanish.
Shifting focus, I
reawaken and struggle
to open my eyes and
see through my blindness.

James Collins

The Unfinished Poem

Just once I'd like to hear
the silver secrets the moon
whispers to water it lays on...

I could never finished this idea.
Chattering information gripped me,
technology engulfed me, work
horded my writing time. But, my
excuses don't change how poetry
is critically needed medicine.
Poetry is a dose of soul.
Words calling us to feel or
open us to a healing.
With ancient roots in imagination
poetry transforms suffering into hope,
allows me to see both the world and
enough unseen meaning to feed
both my heart and spirit.
Like a comet shooting across the
horizons of birth and death, poetry
lifts eyes from the dirt and ties them
to the divine. Or, maybe poetry is a
kite of madness with soulful wings
that undresses what appears to be and
reveals more daring possibilities.

I write about poetry because sometimes
to write poetry is beyond my grasp.
I may capture a scent of its perfume, or
a sweet, first kiss of metaphor, but
by the time I pick up a pen, I feel

like a cave-man with a club.
I sweat and struggle to form words into
lines, and they usually sound like a
child banging on pots and pans.
But like some crazed monkey I have
stuck my hand into a cage of words.

I have been caught.

I have such a firm grip on my yearning
to know what's behind this worldly
veil that I can't let go.
I've been captured by a longing to
write words that can
melt the stars.

James Collins

A Search For Silence

Meditation makes me aware of the
distracting noises of life. Yet,
there could never be a
silence for all occasions.
Not all silences sound the same.

A sun rising kind of hush
glows with a separate frequency
than a shared smile.
Knowing a secret and the
opening of a rose differ from a

jilted lover's disbelief or the
quiet punch of unspoken judgment.
A silent desire speaks louder
than the solemn suffering of wanting.
A slammed door exposes only the

burn of simmering agony.
A shock of loss or the
surprise of grief weighs heavily
on the scales of any heart.
Many remain afraid of even a
casual silence.

Silence is where the
wind comes from and
where it goes.
It's the film soundtrack of
almost every dream.

The moon rises and falls,
waxes and wanes
drenched in it.
Stars twinkle in a dark bowl of
eternal quiet, but I

can't find enough
to finish
my morning
meditation.

James Collins

Beneath the Dusty Relics

Who was Jesus when Christianity was a cult
in those 325 years before the Council of Nicea
obeyed Emperor Constantine, and created
one story to build a church on from
so many cultural versions?
'Divine' is so untouchable.
But, flick away the dust,
there are only questions.

Normally meticulous accountants, Romans
have no record Jesus even existed.
Was he an archetype of the spiritual path
that got personified, and spread like wildfire
in a dry, thirsty material world?
Was the story twisted by theologians,
emperors and church councils?
Do all who seek spirit get crucified?
Can't ask the Arians or Nestorian Christians
outlawed by Nicea. Both sects too were
large to slaughter.

If he really walked the earth,
what did the holy man feel
when the future that once flickered
in his inner eye ended up
bending him under a heavy cross?
Stumbling through a river of dusty
sandals in a burning rain of bloody sweat,
did he experience numbing clouds of pain?
How deeply did he go within himself
to shrink enough to pass through
the eye of the needle.

Could he avoid the jeers, the weeping,
or his own mantra of why me?
Did he float above the tragic scene,
watching and wondering about that
poor slob whipped to raw flesh being
hammered by wooden mallets?
Did he finally recognize the hand
the spike was driving through, or
were his eyes set on the angels
waiting for him to cross over?

James Collins

A Walk in Zen

Even after living like a Zen priest
with no need for answers, a desperate
inner thunder rumbles in the distant
hills of my soul like a far-off storm.
When I walk the sound sometimes
screeches like a red hawk's warning.
Other times, the annoying calamity
is pesky mosquito hum.

I step under a tree and a breeze gently
lifts afternoon leaves and shakes
loose a childhood sadness.
Closing my eyes from that yellow glitter
in the trees, I allow that something lost,
once stuck in time to rise up for release.
Bursting into light from its
grave of memory is my first taste
of that ten cent fudgsicle.

A long forgotten smile shines with
dribbles of melting chocolate.
Knowing this films' ending, there's no
need to brace for the trauma when my cold
glob tumbles off my stick to the ground.
In perfect cosmic segue, my remote noise
turns the corner and becomes an irritating
musical loop of an ice cream vendor.

Opening my eyes, I step to the street,
join a crowd of gathering children.
To honor my inner child, I pay a dollar

for today's fudgsicle, then give a little girl
short a quarter the coin she needed.
Older than yesterday the earth
rolls toward the setting sun, and
in the moment of watching the child
joyfully skip away, my distant
thunder vanishes.

James Collins

Encouragement: Zen Style

I stepped out of the woods
at the end of my street.
A neighbor, trimming his hedge,
waved me over. 'I took your suggestion.
Been asking God to speak to me.'
He soothed his suffering
with a soft demand. 'I really
need to be given a sign.'
A wildly colorful sunset called
the night to come out and play.
A dove cooed softly from a tree.
'How about that?' I said.

Lost in thoughts my neighbor
judged, 'You know, life would make
more sense if God showed himself.'
Maroon spilled across wispy clouds.
The evening star winked from space.
'Check out Venus,' I celebrated.

Clicking his shears in mid-air, 'I'd
like to see even a tiny miracle.'
A doe and her new fawn timidly
risked a shortcut to the brook
behind our cul-de-sac. 'There!'
Not seeing what I saw, he cursed,
'They eat my blooming flowers.'

'I really want my life to change,' he
pressed through a warm emotion
cracking his voice.

44

He rocked for a moment
along that cliff men seldom visit where
tears fall only when no one notices.

'I'm begging God to touch me so I...'
That tear threatened to leap free, he
brushed away a firefly from his forearm,
turned to finish his hedge in the fading light.

Stepping away, I waved and hollered
back to him and all the spirits
reaching out to him. 'Keep trying.'

James Collins

Sharing a Secret

As the pink dawn of your body
spread over me, a few stars
fell from your eyes.
Your warmed-by-passion
voice whispered enough love
to stop my heart beating.
Caught in the soft
glow of candles
the snow of ancient tears
finally
melted down your face.
Wading through the mists
of this old rainbow, I
kissed your face.
White doves, kept hidden
behind your eyes, were
released and flew free
on the silk echo of your
trembling words.
Hesitant with a new hope,
they escaped almost
accidentally from your lips.
By opening this invisible gate
between us, we dissolved in air
where all cloudy secrets were
swept away by a soft sun of trust.
Loosened from the
barriers of skin, I
could not feel where
you began or
I ended.

The Odyssey

A poem is a world brought to
life by a whisper of words.
Good poems beg to be re-read.
Some are a talisman,
others a lucky find.

Rare to read. Rarer to write,
a great poem opens you so
you can read your soul.
I search for them as Ulysses
searched for Ithaca.

Like familiar gods watching
over me, great poems
guide me through any
dark journey, past demons or
a treacherous Cyclops.

To sleep without a lover's
deep kiss is bearable, but
to sleep without a book of
poems in the night stand
within reach is impossible.

Since dreams are the most
real things I know, poetry
like a warrior's shield
protects my vapory visions.

This world is a great dream,
always alive without
beginning or end.
When sirens lure me away
poems call me home.

James Collins

The Saints Say

There's no 'get out of earth free' card,
if you want off the wheel of life.
To run in that holy marathon, the only
escape is to train in the art of meditation.
Easily distracted and tempted,
discipline remains a real challenge.
To log off this body/mind computer, a
spiritual practice takes hard work.
If it was easy, there'd be more than
one Jesus or Buddha.

The saints say
we must die daily to this world and
first seek the kingdom of heaven.
The only way to an island that doesn't
physically exist is to slip into the
silence of inner space.
No matter how hard I swim
against the river of thoughts,
they hold me where I started. But I
learned quieting mental chatter
requires the patience of a saint, AND
that the I am, I am is not physical.

In every dive into the inner ocean,
the mind's inner tube pulls me
back to the surface. But with every
try gentle whispers encourage my soul
to slip back in for another swim.

The saints say
to free the spirit from the body while
in the body is our highest work.
Longing helps my training, and
whether I use the motivational
metaphors of being a student,
a traveler or a prisoner doesn't matter.
God doesn't care how long it takes me.
But, here on earth I know
even my bones are his, and
only borrowed.

James Collins

Acceptance

My father is buried under a bed of blue sky.
He can no longer lift sheets of clouds
to perform any peek-a-boo magic tricks.
And I accept
I may never taste another tomato
under this sun like the ones he grew.
A rumbling, distant thunder could be my
old man snoring or complaining to God
how short life is.
All those evenings he worked, left me with
no memory of his voice saying good night.
Perhaps that was a gift he gave so I could
discover the voice of my inner dad.

My father is buried in my heart where I can't
place any flowers along the strands of my DNA
to soften his stoic John Wayne style.
And I accept
a part of him flows in my dark rivers of blood,
and in hairy roots on my face.
His gruff, enchanting laugh still echoes in
caves and caverns under my skin.
Uncomfortable beads of sweat roll down my
cheeks, reminding me of tears he couldn't cry.

My father is buried in this ground, and there's
no magic ladder to climb down to hear
his Archie Bunker advice.
So I accept
he can't make the grave into his home with
unlocked doors and his famous shrimp Creole.

My shadow falls across his grave, and
moments tick and tock like a soundtrack
in a Bergman film.
Now, I hear those boring, yet deadly
bombs of time approaching. Tick. Tock.

If his spirit can watch the souls he created
who still run on this playground, I
hope he accepts how the angels might
teach him to do better. And, if he takes
a moment to look through the veil, sees me
still tossing my music into the air,
knows he did all right.

James Collins

In the Wild

I ride a pickup now instead of a pony, and
live within the great trinity of
Inner child
Man and
Elder.

I fly deep into the dark woods with gray owl feathers
in my hair. My hungry feet sink in
this old earth
like new
roots.

I sit alone with dancing shadows of a campfire,
feeling inner echoes of deep longing,
a call for
my spirit
to blaze!

I hear a moaning wind rustle Aspen leaves as Cherokee
ghosts gather to sit with me under this
night's blanket
with flames
crackling.

I listen to their holy presence as silvery clouds of men
speak like the poetry of smoke about
their own time
as skin
walkers.

I dance in my holy moments of flesh, floating
like flickering embers tossed about on the wind.
Sparks of my
heart in
the wild.

James Collins

Cry this Tear

Slowly our eyes are wrapped with
blindfolds of thoughts and beliefs.
With blinders properly in place, we
become good, obedient children.
Once bound, we slowly forget
our source and essence.

It's no wonder when careening
down this wild river of life, we
yearn for any calm, blissful stillness.
If an ancient mystic calls
from the river's edge, he's trying
to awaken you from your trance.
Listen when he reminds you to toss
ambition overboard and to follow the
rainbow to that pot of golden spirit
before your boat goes over the falls.

But the mind has us busy rowing madly.
If wise, scream for help. But anyone
holy will only toss you a rope made of
moonlight and misty meditations.
Only those who have tried all things
and remain unsatisfied will ever
grab such a fragile line.
Once we hold this vaporous rope,
it tugs and turns us within. Blindfolds
and separation dissolves.

The one within begins to reveal
the true I am, and the sacred
drop of spirit starts to shine.
In the very moment we decide to cling
to spirit's life preserver, angels run to us,
gather and kneel all around us, waiting
to catch the most precious jewel
in all the world —
a tear that longs for God.

James Collins

The Stranger

In the beginning young fathers
hold and carry a hopeful love.
When he comes home his young children
run to greet, play and tickle. But,
life has many openings and closings of doors,
of hearts. Drop by drop moments
collect into years. Breath by breath, fathers
weary of the separation from all he loves.

He's set apart by time clocks,
pay checks and bills – seldom his own.
Fathers spend their lives hunting
for worthless, green paper that never piles
high enough to matter or to mend
the lost time in connecting his heart to
the eyes within the soul of his child.
Something in him withers in the missed
laughter, pitches not thrown, drawings
not colored, stories not read.

These losses haunt the house of his heart.
Leaves don't shimmer with joy
in the wind, sunsets no longer stir wonder.
One day he arrives home with his
exhausted temperament and leaking soul.
Blank stares that barely lift themselves
off the TV screen greet him.

His kids are older, lost behind mountains of
homework, or out playing with friends.
This is the fragile moment no one notices
when a man's heart slowly begins
to bleed.

He winces but says nothing. Now,
the real work begins.

How a father keeps his soul from turning
numb or bitter as he sees his love
lost in the shadows that pass
so quickly in his own home
without him.

James Collins

One Morning

The alarm clock terrorized me awake.
Turning it off, I swung feet to the floor in
the silvery steel seeping through my window.
Greeting the shadows with a sigh, I staggered
to the bathroom like a lost, absent-minded
professor without his coffee cup compass.

Face the mirror. Get it over with.
Will I see someone I know today?
Where's that young, idealistic man?
Surprised by the stranger in the mirror,
curiosity pushed me to peek again.
Who is this with the graying tousled hair?

Would my life be different, if I had asked
my first love not to leave when she visited
me that summer after she graduated?
What stopped me from stopping her? In the
face of all others, I've never felt at home.

Memory's winding streets and dead-end alleys
didn't release any more haunting ghosts.
Remembering only pushed away a cold truth:
I face a stranger every morning, and
none will be 25 again.

Beyond this reflection, behind the image,
buried within the puzzle of personality,
my soul waits.
Asking no more awkward questions, I
foam and shave today's face with slow,

trust building deliberation. Then, this
stranger in my mirror freely speaks
like every small town gossip.

> 'Love isn't out there in the world, you know.
> Nope. Not anywhere. Love begins here. In
> these eyes. When you can look here and say
> I love you, you invite your soul to show up.
> Begin a new life. It's never too late. Quit
> searching. Stop waiting. Just say it.'

The alarm clock terrorized me awake one morning.

James Collins

A Writer's Cluttered Desk

Mounds of notes, rolling hills of ring binders and
pyramids of scribbled ideas made up
the landscape of my desk.
A challenge pressed me into those shifting sands
to discover what was buried there.
By clearing the loose scraps one at a time, I hoped
to avoid a messy literary landslide.

Exploring the towering temples, I excavated a
tunnel where veins of ink were written so fast
they trailed off into unreadable hieroglyphics.
Like symbols from ancient tombs, I found messages
from a struggling musician, the wounded lover,
that lonesome warrior, a shadowy magician and
a prince destined to be king.

I struck a mother lode in a collapsing cavern along
paper timbers of a lost mine, a rich vein of song lyrics.
In the gold rush panic I mishandled a stick of dynamite.
Reading those old words lit a split second fuse. But,
before the explosion killed me all over again,
a grey whiskered prospector waved me back, hollering
'Jumpin' Jehoshaphat' and one 'By Jiminy'.
The flash came, dust settled and, thanks to the inner
old-timer's warning, almost all my fragments
magically returned me to my original form.

That unearthed holy relic was a raw truth written
in tiny drops of blood, a necklace of rubies
spattered on the wrinkled skin of a dead tree.
A deep longing stuck in the echoes of unkept promises.

Like a Mayan altar after a sacrifice, the
desk held my freshly cut heart
still throbbing with hope for her love.

Better left buried, ghosts swirled in
cursed memories
of kisses that rattled my bones.
Escaping the Tasmanian tornado, I backed out,
clutching my fragments together, and
scrawled a new sign over this room.

> Messy piles of paper act like a
> writer's bullet proof vest.
> If you see an old prospector
> waving his arms, and me running out,
> catch up.
> Something's been disturbed
> on a writer's cluttered desk.

James Collins

A Secret even to Me

I can't describe the longing to
feel my bare feet on the earth.
Half my energy pours
from my heart through my
body into this skin of dirt.

The rest of me explodes into
my crown and sails into heaven.
In the center is a love song.
God-given I'm told, but buried
so deep it's a secret even to me.

A honey of silence flows through
me to sweeten all sorrows.
It finds endless places to grow,
rises up in wild places and
at wild times.

Every drop of silence is a seed
that falls on the ground
under my feet to lift me up.
But, when I open my mouth
to sing, I never find the song
my heart longs to express.

That's ok, I sing anyway. But,
by this point in time, my
guess is this God-given
song of mine is silence.
Now that would be
God's kind of joke.

The Difference

A break-up is when
someone you love and trust
drops your heart on the floor
to shatter in a million pieces, and
then walks out, leaving you
in the angst of either chasing
after them, or doing the work
to put yourself back together.

A divorce is when
someone you love and trust
slowly pulls barbed wire
through your heart, and kicks
the life out of your soul, until
all that's left is an empty wallet.

Then they turn back on you
with some mad pit bull who
carries a briefcase of demands
in his teeth.

James Collins

Reading Life's Punctuation

Pushing around nouns and verbs at work,
I stare out my window at the bold
asterisks of naked winter trees.
Their stiff language references
another season passing me by.
In the twisted twigs of quotation marks,
I hear holy promises, not yet spoken
and the wind whispers gracefully
about a freedom I'll never know.

A soft, gleaming arrow shines
through that same crowd of trees when
dipped in the green ink of spring.
During a sunlit exclamation point, I
break for lunch where I see a gold light
pour through the eye of a cloud. Leaving
the sidewalk café, a scattering rush of
pigeons lift into flight. In an epiphany
I catch what is written by feathers
as I reenter the cage of my office.

Across a summer sky as I leave for home,
pages of a dazzling rainbow flutter,
daring me to feel childish wonder.
Any essence of wild abandon is written
by passing footsteps running to a lover
on a rainy sidewalk. Splashing through
puddles of guilt without stopping
for a selfish decaf may be as close
to love as some souls get.

Later when their naked hips float
in a pool of silk sheets soft moans will
whisper under a sliver of moon
with clouds hanging on it.

It's clear to me tonight that life
is the language of God.
Each soul is a writing tool,
creating a story, fumbling with
a lame alphabet and crude syllables.

I still don't understand the grammar,
grasp the part of speech I am, or
the meaning my sentence adds
to this brief paragraph of time.
I turn down my bed,
tired of not hearing
from my circle of angels.
If they're trying to reach me,
they must be writing on smoke.

In the whimsical slang of dreams,
I wrestle wild words
in the holy cage of forever,
but I can't coax them into
any autobiography where love
is the only theme that makes sense.

I sit in my dream and
break pencils in frustration
because
when awake,
life writes so easily
about love with
the simple wings of a butterfly.

James Collins

Moment By Moment

Authors and gurus praise the art of presence.
'Being in the now' is an easy seduction to sip,
a way of savoring the fruity wine of forever.
Meditating for years. I still stagger around
drunk on distractions, stumbling through time.
My martini of mind shakes me out of most
moments to chase thoughts that
scatter like leaves in the wind.

I guzzle gobs of time wondering what to fix
for breakfast, or do with a fresh Saturday. It's
to hot cut the grass. Cleaning? Yeah, right.
After granola in coconut milk and almond
buttered toast with black raspberry jam, I'm
in a narrow tunnel between past and future.
A moment with nothing to do.

My inner rebel fights times' tight fitting
clothes, so I grab the keys to run errands.
Starting the car begins a new age seminar.
But to answer why the radio was that loud
focuses on the past. Free from daily chores,
my inner laziness giggles as I flow down
streets in a river of time until a truckload of
crazy thoughts crashes my trance.

That old, lone gunman, magic bullet and
lame cover-up for the Kennedy Coup de tat.
There's no easy way out when thoughts
chase me into a box canyon.

I turn the radio louder to quiet my struggle
to stay present. Deep breaths don't mend
my love/hate relationship with time.
With all this grabbing on and letting go
I do, I'm a trapeze artist without a net,
lost, swinging moment by moment.

James Collins

Once Married to Madness

The dark twin of a full moon slowly rose.
Like an eerie breeze wailing whispers
from gathering banshees floated in the air.
Copper demons pressed so hard against
the veil of life that the friction between
the seen and unseen worlds created a
smoky iridescence, a blinding haze, a
hypnotic, opal fog of unconsciousness.
A mob of black shadows crowded
around our house so chaotically
my own angels couldn't find me.
Like a murky ooze of high tide, a soft
craziness drifted in unnoticed...until she
said, 'Let's take Jeremy off your will.'
I pretended not to hear, but the first
real fear for my life bubbled up.

With her maniacal sleeplessness I
separated to the upstairs bedroom.
I placed noise makers by the door
in case she opened it while I slept.
A silver dust of perpetual midnight
settled on the furniture.
When the darkness landed on the hearts
of the children, I rubbed enough ash from
my eyes to watch a small hate from her
troubled mind destroy our family.
Awakening too late, I couldn't stop the
collapse of my small part of the world.
My trembling grief took years to heal, but I
found here in my heart, not in someone else's,

was the only place love could ever call home.
On the day I climbed out from the rubble,
a fragile flame flickered in my soul.
I waited for a sun to rise that would
fill me with the light of love again.
Then, blowing the dust off old dreams, I
continued my journey.

James Collins

The Shaman in Albertson's

Shivering, my feet crunch in the snow as I
stumble through my shattered life.
On my way to Albertson's the shallow graves
of my ghostly footsteps weave a teardrop trail.

Still in shock from a karmic ambush, I'm
homeless. Day 14. Taos, New Mexico. A
Saturday. Early January. Bracing against a wind,
the hand in my coat pocket clings

to one last thread of sanity. This key unlocks a
heated jobsite trailer where I sometimes sleep.
I grasp the thin brass jewel with the tenderness
of someone very near the end of his rope.

Some say when moments turn into minutes
is a sacred time, but betrayal's dagger cuts deep.
My wife has energetically murdered me, and
my spirit still bleeds from this wound.

Under another spell of copper poisoning she
won't snap out of this one and apologize.
Hungry for truth, I've lost 25 pounds.
Today, I'm buying frozen dinners to

store in the snow. I first saw the Shaman in
Albertson's shuffling up to me through an
open cooler's glass door. The old Indian
asked some invisible companion,

'Is this the one? You need healing. Come.
To the reservation. Tomorrow.' I looked
around to see who he was speaking to,
'You. You come. In a holy place. I explain.'

The next day we sat in rickety wooden chairs.
He rattled for a few minutes, chanted some
doubts away, then gathered words like
precious stones. 'You, white wolf.

Strong medicine. Wounded Healer. There's a
vortex on this reservation. Called the dweller
on the threshold. Anyone in this energy not
living his real life gets torn up and shredded.
Your woman is that dark arrow.
This is spirit's gift. A new birth.
No longer her pack mule.
You are free. Clear of her lies.'

Maybe I nodded before surrendering to a
river of soothing tears. The soft screech
of his chair told me the shaman stood.
'Brother, it's hard for a wolf

to lose his family. In holy aloneness,
gently heal yourself. Stop carrying
the burdens of others. Live your real life.
Travel well. Stand tall.'

By the time I took my head
out of my hands, he was gone, and
the long, hard road of healing
my wounded soul began.

James Collins

The Masquerade Party

Life is God's masquerade party.
We attend in our disguises,
play with trinkets or beg
party favors while we whine
about the karmic cheese we eat.
Yet, no one wants to be the first
to take off their costume.

> Undress the gaudy ego, loosen
> the belts of a crisp persona, unravel
> from the fashions of Aries or Gemini.
> Get real and raw. Lose the mask.

Ah, the mind is always restless, tosses
out wild warnings, buries us in worry
and reasons to stay in the pretense.

> Learn to ignore them.
> Attend to the heart.
> When the heart sings with the soul,
> spirit composes a song so joyful,
> you will never stop living.

We are the pen in God's hand,
so write what whispers in your heart.
Put your spirit on each
passing page of life. At least,
take the cap off the pen and
let your light loose on a world
so badly in need of love.

And with this pen of light write
about your longing for spirit, for
life without the mask, for love
in divine capital letters.

God searches his cluttered
desk of life for any human
who can write the one,
true purpose with their
rattling pages of breath.

    Write with the ink of who you really are.
    Then watch how God will pour
    through your eyes and how the whole
    earth will move and shake.

To give up our disguise
is the purpose for this party.
Ah, but the restless mind is afraid.

    Push it aside and write
    your love story with spirit,
    not with wanting.

Learn to let God speak through you
until you can say,
I am a spirit expressing love.

Landscapes

All horizons are the bodies of my children,
laying asleep somewhere far away.
A mix of forest green and brave brown
remind me of one child's eyes, and the
innocent shades of sky reflect another.

Dressed in the deep blue of distant love
those hills are the colors of my longing.
A thin strata of clouds hold
untouchable reminisces of happier
days I can not reach.

The memories I carry, but dare not open,
make me an immigrant wandering to new
places, and nowhere ever feels like home.
I can't forget my heart's loss
when the eruptions of dark hate and

copper lava spread their shadowy fire
over the true story.
That volcano changed the landscapes
of sweet, tender souls, altering
all they would become.

None of my wishing it was different
can change that now, so I pray
that the soul star in each
child finds a way to shine.
Every night on the edges of sleep

in a ghostly mist of tears, I
whisper good night to them.
When an echo bounces
back from the dark landscape,
telling me to trust, I

wrestle with that angel until I
fall into a wisdom of grief
I have yet to
understand.

James Collins

My Epitaph

Another karma crash and I'm in a
New Age workshop trying to heal myself.
I know there's little truth in advertising but
becoming an angel in a once a month
seminar could happen. But, all my

years on the bottom of this ocean of air
outfitted with the standard, deep dimensional
diving equipment of body and ego, I
don't see how I'll ever fly with wings
that look more like dented fenders.

Somewhere in the fumes of becoming
an angel and my skepticism, I sat in the class.
Last month's lesson was healing the fear of death.
She approached the subject as gentle as a ghost.
The homework was to write my own epitaph.

That death happens to others is a human
delusion my ego perpetuates. But I read
Pierre Teilhard de Chardin in the 70's, and truly
believe I'm a spirit having a human experience.

As each person recites their words, I'm
impressed with the poetic and poignant phrases.
Terror begins to gnaw at my persona
with every new etching
spoken by the voices on paper stones.

Silence delivers a gentle panic attack
called - it must be my turn.
With angelic compassion the teacher says,
'So Jamie, I walk up to your tombstone.
Tell me what I see carved in the granite that
rests on the top of your grave.'

Taking a deep breath, I read,
I am Not Here.

James Collins

My Healing Angel

Years after our college romance, marriages to
separate strangers and divorces, I
bumped into my healing angel.
Recovering from life's tilt-a whirl ride, I heard
a whisper, 'Any moment of love is precious.'

So tonight she is the star I wish on.
She rises from the satin sheets like a goddess,
glowing with serene, nurturing passion.
She colors me with the touch of her
whisper in tones so soothing that I
gasp and weep with wanting.
I hold her closer than breath to better
hear the heavenly curse of her naked voice.

The sensual sighs of her music fill my heart.
Innocent whispers and spiritual echoes
fall gently on me as we swim in the sacred
pool where right and wrong, and
guilt or shame disappear.
Face to face with forever is always
love's hope, but seldom realized.
My tongue surrounds her breast as I
completely trust in the wisdom of now.

Once again our hearts are in one river,
flowing over each other like
waves searching for a shore.
When her soft moons hum in the full
fever of surrender, I sip her spirit like
a wine that whispers secrets to me.

We paint the essence of dreams with
moonlight brushes and touch the
canvas of life in a way that makes
the giving and the gift sacred.

After being bound by time and God's trials,
she unlocks my shackles and guides a
river of healing love to quench the
desert my heart has become
after so long without her.

James Collins

Three Crows

On a clear, early spring morning a
blazing blue sky
bids for my attention.
My eyes wander to the top branches of a
bright green sugar maple.

Along the rim of new leaves
sit three black crows.
The tight group sways.
Black fluorescent wings
ripple in the breeze.

They sit in quiet knowing.
Beaks remain still.
None sing or caw.

Is this silence the business of brothers, or
secret tactics of a
blackbird brotherhood?

Do they sense any difference among them?
Hold a prejudice for sparrows or cardinals?
How easily they forget a
nest of twigs, and any
history with mom and dad.

They live with no past, and so, they fly free.
With no evidence they are flappingly
glad winter is over, I

wonder if they hold any sense of time,
of passing, or of dreams?
If they possess no reasons or excuses,
do these birds hold anything

beyond instinct?
One by one the crows fly
off. Perhaps, they know
gratitude.

James Collins

Advice for Future Prophets

Beware prophet
when you step on these city streets.
You'll be lost among wide-eyed crazies,
panhandlers and rumpled, rabid homeless.
Here in a maze of avenues, we are
separated from the God of nature, and
trapped in the menagerie of mind.

Modern humans are
tightly tucked into suits of self pity.
Any dose of fear or doom will fail.
After trying to turn stony faces
away from their electronic gadgets,
you may notice how even the leaves
begin to tremble about our future.

Better to call yourself
Jesus, but be prepared to show a passport.
Love is the precious raindrop in this desert.
Or, have a miracle or two handy because
where sleeping souls walk on dark streets,
a tender unwrapping may gather a few hearts.
Remind us how a dove coos, the shy deer

nibbles on curiosity,
how the river flows and trees grip the
earth to serve us air, or how clouds never die
as they whisper to us to keep dreaming.
Our naked souls only twinkle when
inspired or stunned by awe.
Ask softly, no, invite us into our hearts

by introducing us
to the reverence of a rose opening.
Don't tell those asleep that they can wake up
or you'll be asking for serious trouble.
Never tell those awake that they are asleep
because that will only place you in danger.
Maybe, if your voice is gentle, and

we don't kill you,
you'll help us discover why our hearts fail us
when the very life of this earth is at stake.
Truth be told, saving us from ourselves
won't be easy.

James Collins

Presence

Presence is a pure flame
that rises to both fill and
consume every moment of air.
It touches life with sparks of joy and
ignites spirit to subdue
personality
with a voice that has
no need for wisdom
because love is the song
on every breath.

Then the lungs in a man's chest
filled with the heart of a child
heaves to catch enough air to
laugh with the
exploding
embers
of a soul
set free.

Wondering Where the Lions Are

When the soft, heartbeat thunder
drifted into silence my rapture
in the divine bubble ended.
Leaving the cave of love, I
chased that hypnotic sound, but
a worldly web wrapped me
in an unconscious coma.
Wounded by thorns of fear, I hid
until my numbness felt like comfort.

Sleepwalking through this jungle
in a new suit of skin, I wandered
lost on the Serengeti, in wild places,
gathering a herd of dead dreams to tend.
My safari crept through a desert
on the dead side of love, often in circles,
along old, rusty chain link reasons, but
every step into thirst quenching

addictions pulled me deeper
into a hellish hunger.
Suffering and blaming
helped me ignore any pesky
whispers from an unseen God.
By not opening my eyes I
held the trance in place, and
buried myself in dark, sleepy fears
to hide from the winds of change.

James Collins

Yet, a jungle part of me
danced and rattled, chanting
like a demonic shaman. But,
rather than awakening, I

pretended to stay safe,
remaining captive.
I tended my herd of dead dreams,
played with old bones and never
heard the grass crackle.

Smelling the scent of easy prey,
circling predators gathered.
Claws eager to maul my mask
whisked the air around me.
Distant drums beat steadily in my head,
'Wake up!'
Within my shepherd boy persona,
a lost man started to stir.

The low grumbling growls circled closer.
I blinked an eye awake only
to misinterpret their distance.
Even if I let these lions
take their share, I can't escape.

A strange calm tightened
around my soul.
Sniffing whiskers trembled
against my skin.
Waiting until these snarling
jowls of my own demons
surrounded me, God
released the lions of love.

They tore me from my
dead dreams
limb by limb,
scattered pieces of me
everywhere and

left me with nothing but
empty hands, a prayer and the
chance to build a new life
with only love.

By waiting for the cosmic 2x4
to strike, I paid a high price
for this gift, but
am no longer
wondering
where the lions are.

James Collins

As Fall Turns to Winter

No one genuflects as they enter
the Church of Radnor Lake, but this
morning my spirit does a secret dance.
Most of the leafy walls have fallen, exposing
the bare bone architecture of brown trees.

Reverently, I watch a few lingering leaves cling
to what's known, then float into the unknown.
Every dazzling dive of surrender dances
with joyful sorrow in autumn's air.

This ritual of release is the leap of faith we
all must make one day. So I am
blessed to walk between life and death.

In a sacred temple parishioners take communion
wafers quietly, and bond with their soul.
Visitors huff and puff by me with the world
still stuck in their ears. Others disregard
psalms of silence and connect in conversation.

From a branch-in-the-water pew, a turtle,
listens to a cool sun's sermon on patience.
A sparkling congregation of diamonds rise on
the lake before him in waves of Hallelujah.

Along the path, a twisted tree trunk's nine inch
gnarl invites me to wonder what grace straightened
it again to reach for the sun and sway contentedly.
Geese glide on the lake, sharing the message of
their ministry – to be in the world, not of the world.

In a creek a blue heron is baptized.
From a hillside altar, a deer's peaceful presence
preaches to be gentle with myself. The natural love
in this moment quiets my mind and heart.

Staring in this stain glass mystery, I pray
that God is alive within and all around us,
that we won't wait until the last tree is cut, or
the last river is poisoned to realize the
harm we do, that being human means to honor

life over money and profits, that
in our season of living in this human
tabernacle, a thin root of breath, this
fragile thread holds me on the tree of life.

If nature is a mirror, then this is not
my day to dance into the unknown, but
to embrace
the changing seasons of my life
as fall turns to winter.